CHRISTMAS ON THE JAZZY SIDE

11 Elementary to Late Elementary Piano Arrangements in 5-Finger Position
with Jazz-Style Teacher Duets

Sharon Aaronson

The best part of Christmas is gathering together with family and friends to celebrate the season. Playing the carols in *Christmas on the Jazzy Side* is a wonderful way for students and their teachers or parents to enjoy spending time together during the holidays.

Students parts are written in 5-finger position (except for *Silent Night*, which requires a slight shift in the left hand). For ease in reading, the single-line melody is divided between the hands and is written on the grand staff. Only simple rhythms are found in the carols, which also contains lyrics for singing.

Duet parts are fun for the teacher or a more advanced player, and they appeal to developing students. The refreshing jazz harmonies in the accompaniments complement the melodies while providing rhythmic support. Among the various styles are swing bass (*Up on the Housetop*), Latin (*God Rest Ye Merry, Gentlemen*), jazz waltz (*We Wish You a Merry Christmas*), ballad (*Silent Night*) and pop (*Angels We Have Heard on High*).

I hope that you enjoy your holidays on the jazzy side this and every year. Merry Christmas!

Sharon Aaronson

Angels We Have Heard on High	14
Away in a Manger	12
First Noel, The	4
God Rest Ye Merry, Gentlemen	18
Jingle Bells	22
Joy to the World	6
Silent Night	16
Up on the Housetop	10
We Three Kings	8
We Wish You a Merry Christmas	2
What Child Is This?	20

D1416127

Cover art: Dana D'Elia

WE WISH YOU A MERRY CHRISTMAS

Traditional
Arr. by Sharon Aaronson

* Play the eighth notes a bit unevenly:

long short long short

DUET PART: (Student plays one octave higher.)

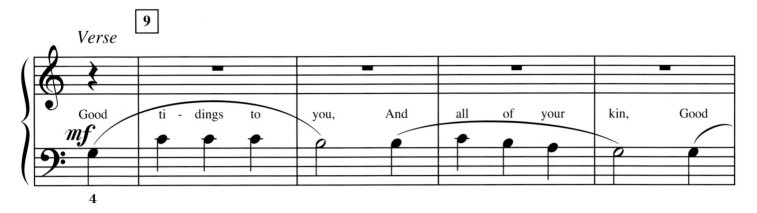

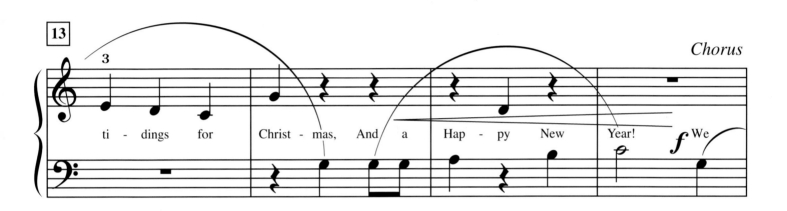

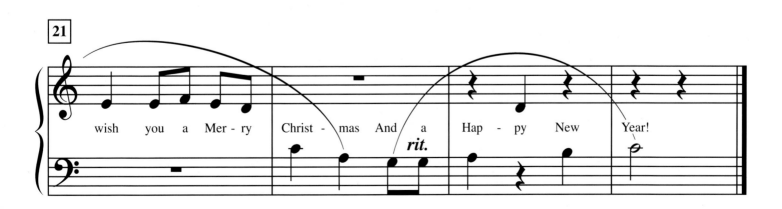

THE FIRST NOEL

English Traditional
Arr. by Sharon Aaronson

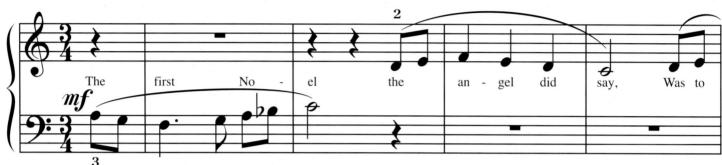

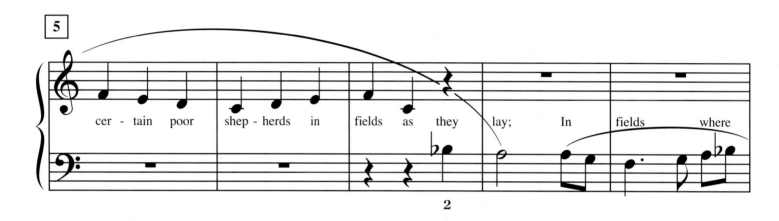

DUET PART: (Student plays one octave higher.)

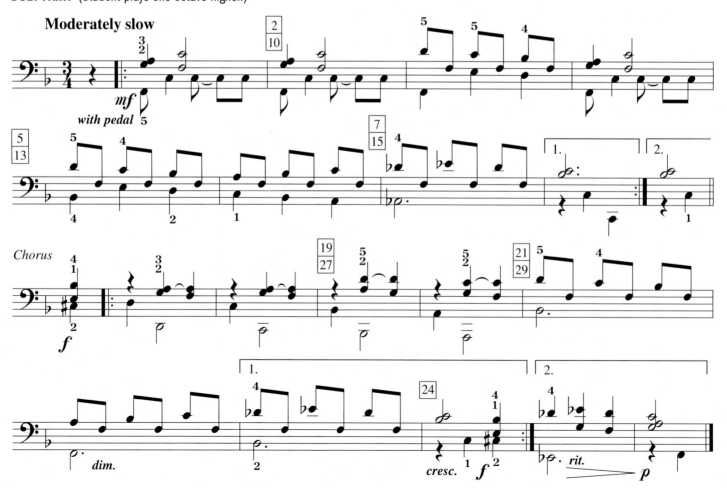

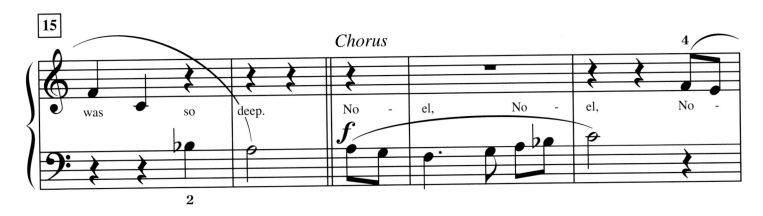

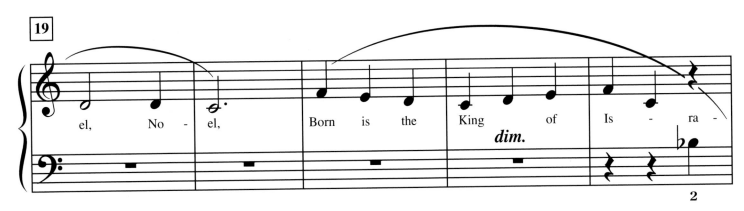

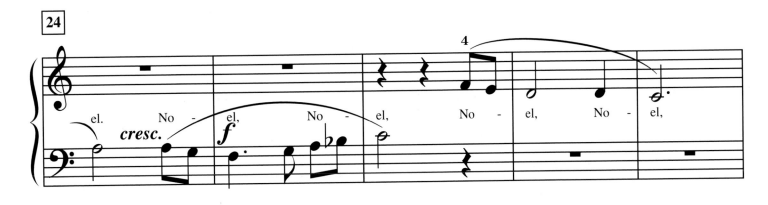

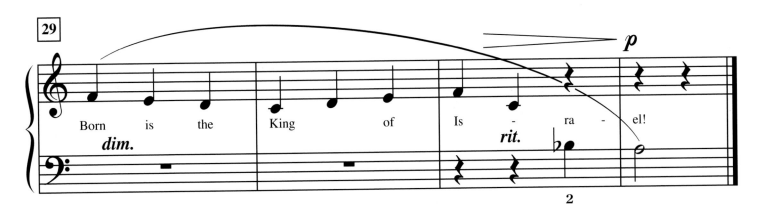

JOY TO THE WORLD

George F. Handel

Arr. by Sharon Aaronson

DUET PART: (Student plays one octave higher.)

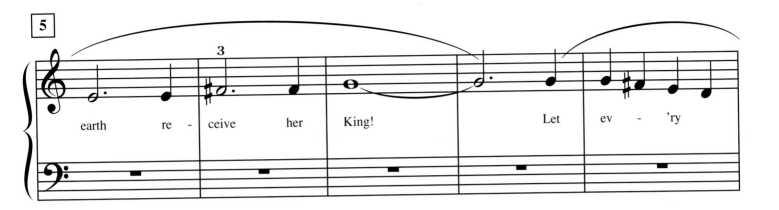

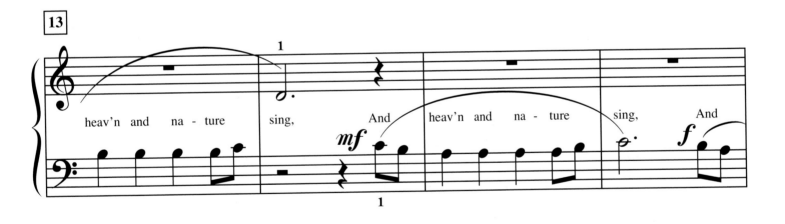

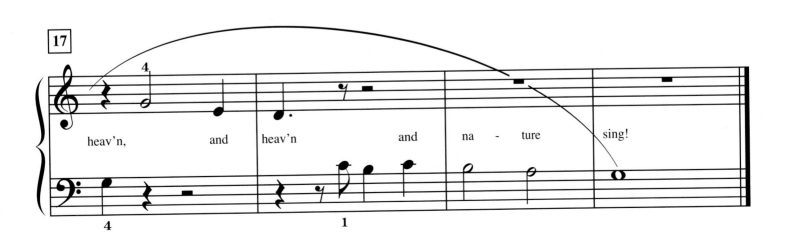

WE THREE KINGS

John Henry Hopkins
Arr. by Sharon Aaronson

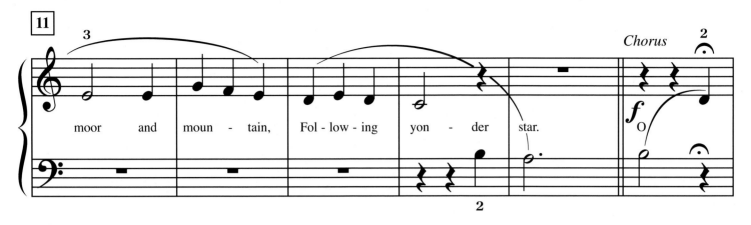

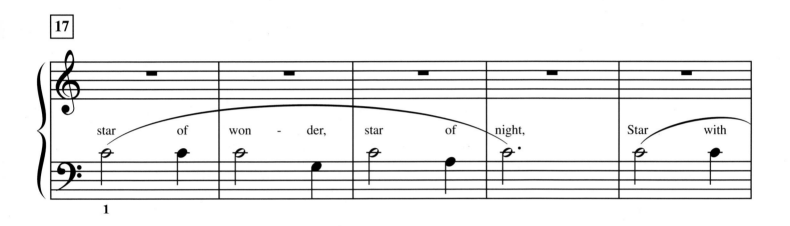

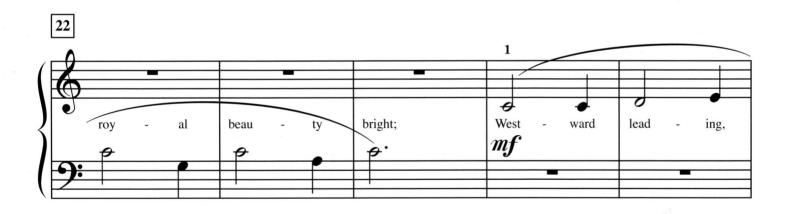

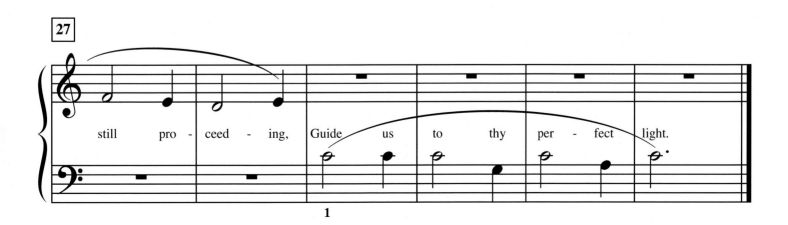

UP ON THE HOUSETOP

B. R. Handy
Arr. by Sharon Aaronson

* Play the eighth notes a bit unevenly:

long short long short

DUET PART: (Student plays one octave higher.)

AWAY IN A MANGER

James R. Murray

Arr. by Sharon Aaronson

DUET PART: (Student plays one octave higher.)

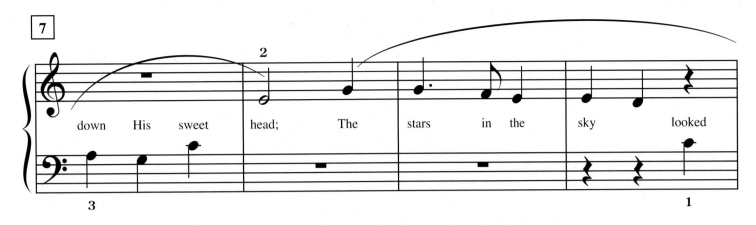

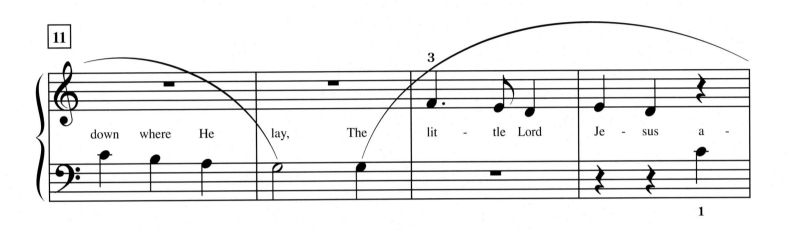

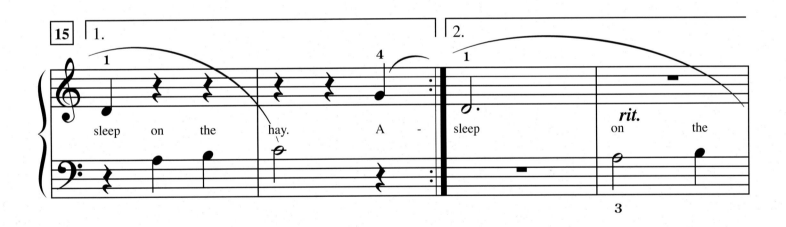

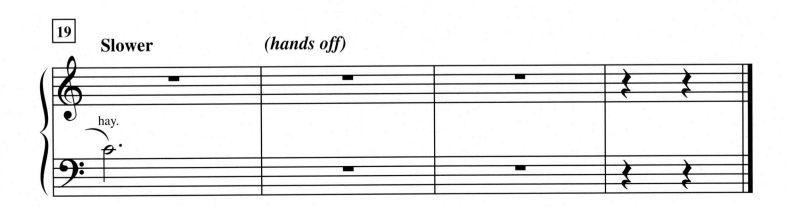

ANGELS WE HAVE HEARD ON HIGH

French Carol
Arr. by Sharon Aaronson

With spirit

An - gels we have heard on high, Sweet - ly sing - ing o'er the plains,

DUET PART: (Student plays one octave higher.)

With spirit *(even eighths)*

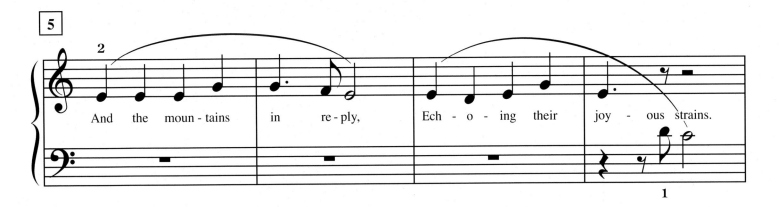

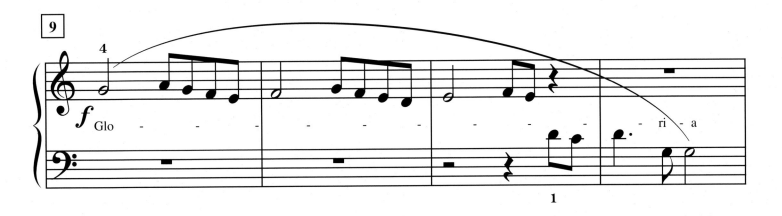

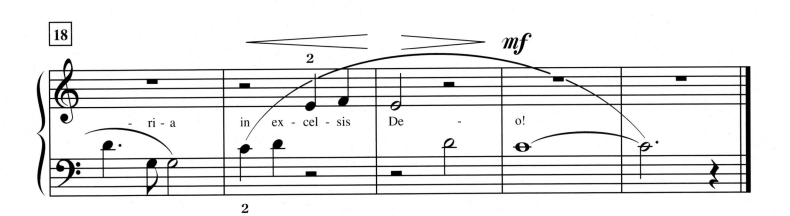

SILENT NIGHT

Franz Gruber
Arr. by Sharon Aaronson

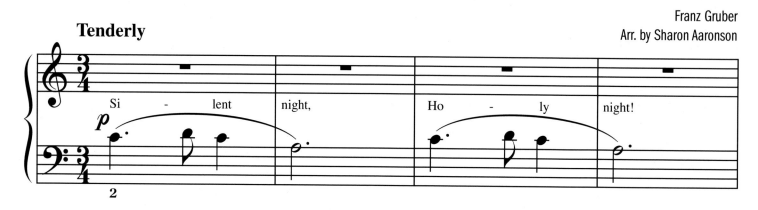

Tenderly

Si - lent night, Ho - ly night!

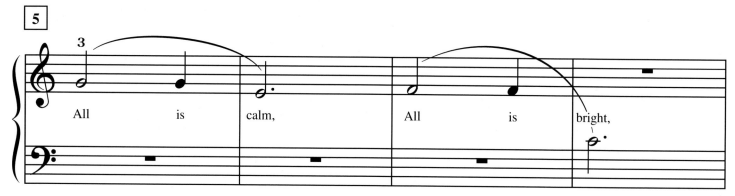

All is calm, All is bright,

DUET PART: (Student plays one octave higher.)

Tenderly

with pedal

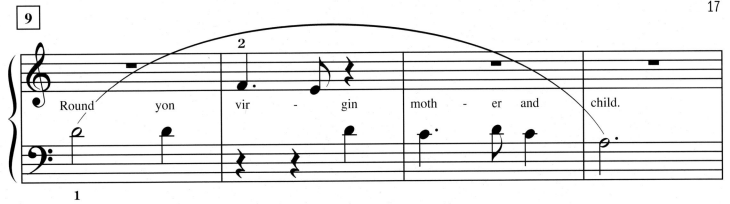

Round yon vir - gin moth - er and child.

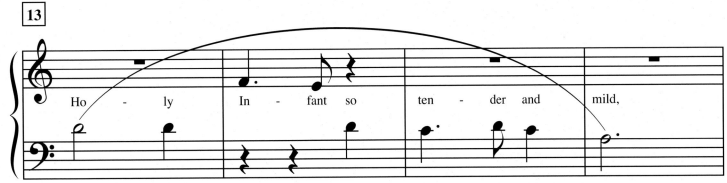

Ho - ly In - fant so ten - der and mild,

Sleep in heav - en - ly peace,

Sleep in heav - en - ly peace.

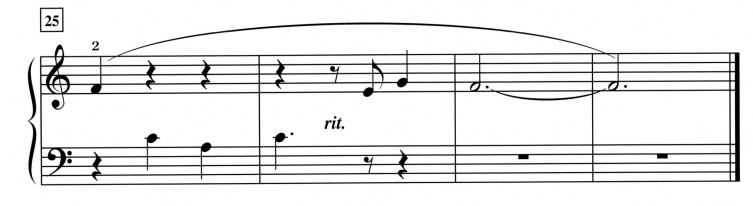

rit.

GOD REST YE MERRY, GENTLEMEN

English Traditional
Arr. by Sharon Aaronson

DUET PART: (Student plays one octave higher.)

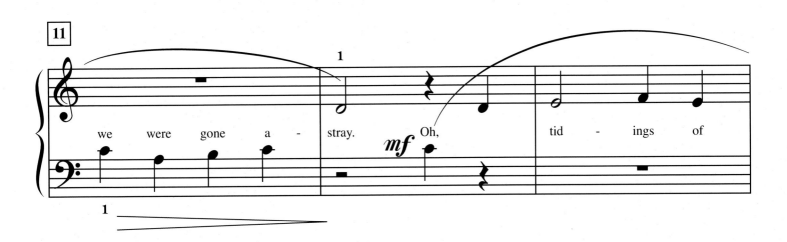

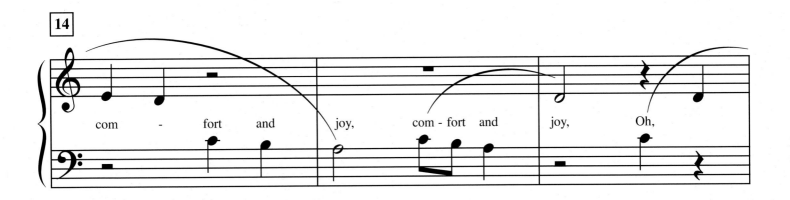

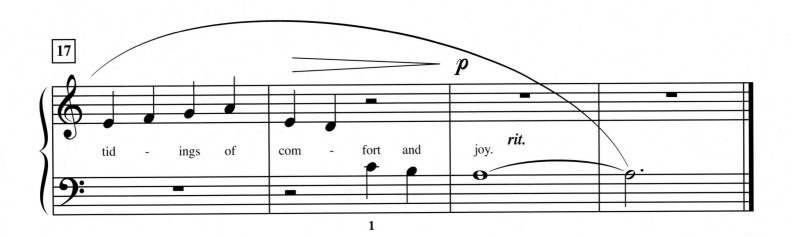

WHAT CHILD IS THIS?

Old English Melody

Arr. by Sharon Aaronson

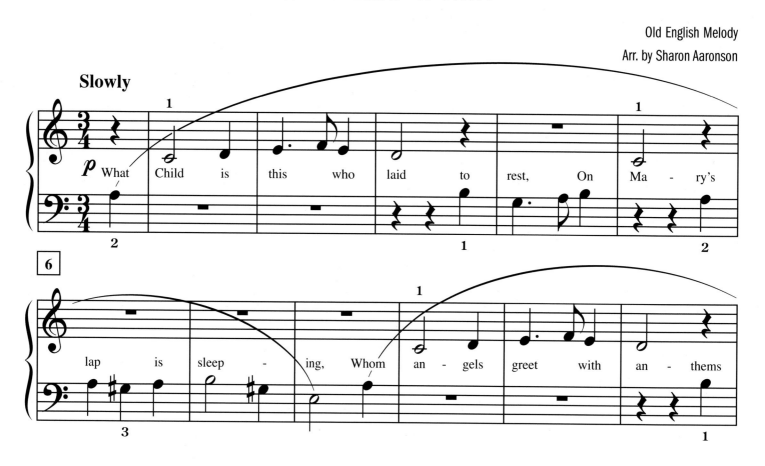

Slowly

p What Child is this who laid to rest, On Ma - ry's

6 lap is sleep - ing, Whom an - gels greet with an - thems

DUET PART: (Student plays one octave higher.)

Slowly *(even eighths)*

p *with pedal*

(jazz eighths ♫ = 𝅘𝅥𝅮 𝅘𝅥𝅮)

mf

(even eighths)

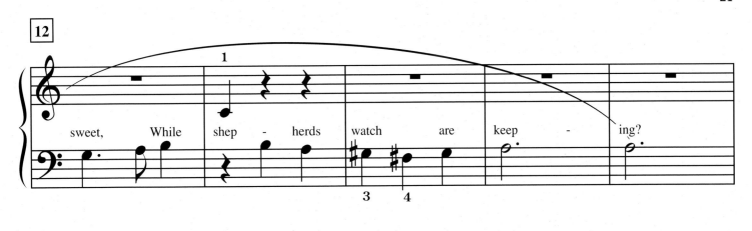

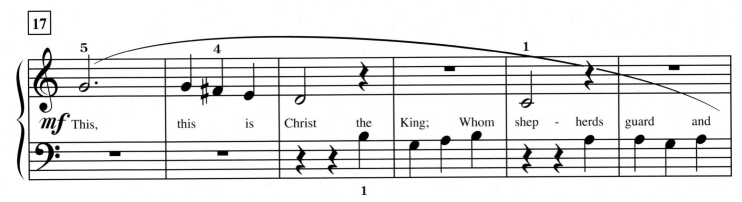

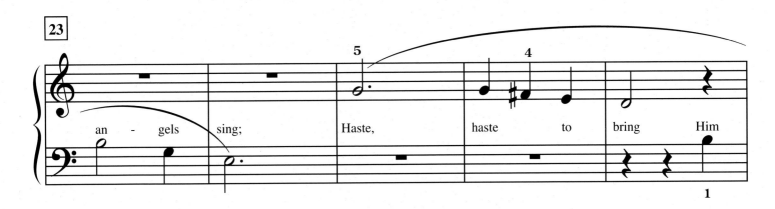

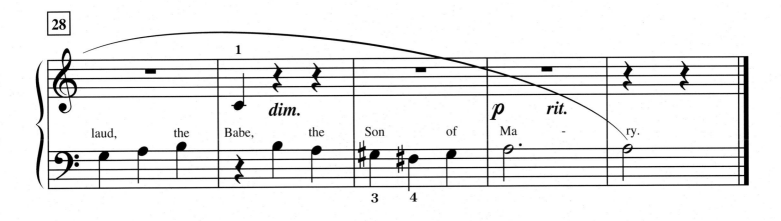

JINGLE BELLS

James Pierpont
Arr. by Sharon Aaronson

Happily

Dash - ing through the snow   In a   one - horse o - pen   sleigh,

DUET PART: (Student plays one octave higher.)

Happily (Latin)

25

f Jin - gle bells! Jin - gle bells! Jin - gle all the way!

29

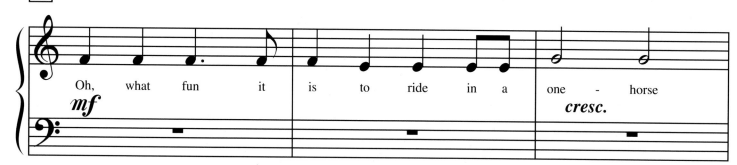

Oh, what fun it is to ride in a one - horse

mf *cresc.*

32

Play 3 times:
1st time as written
2nd time one octave higher
3rd time two octaves higher

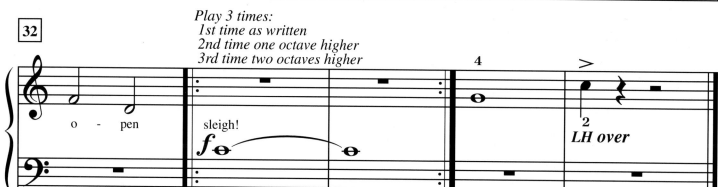

o - pen sleigh! *f* LH over

DUET PART

CHRISTMAS PIANO MUSIC *from Alfred*

Christmas Collections

Early Elementary
Christmas Carol Activity Book, Pre-Reading *(Kowalchyk/Lancaster)* 18197
Christmas Festival, Book 1 *(Kowalchyk/Lancaster)* 6012
My First Christmas Carols *(Kowalchyk/Lancaster)* 233

Early Elementary/Elementary
Christmas Carol Activity Book 1 *(Kowalchyk/Lancaster)* 18198

Elementary
Christmas Festival, Book 2 *(Kowalchyk/Lancaster)* 6044
First Favorite Christmas Carols *(Olson)* 2539
Simply Classic Christmas, A *(Goldston)* 17384

Elementary/Late Elementary
Christmas on the Jazzy Side *(Aaronson)* 19746
Simply Classic Nutcracker, A *(Goldston)* 18077

Late Elementary
Christmas Festival, Book 3 *(Kowalchyk/Lancaster)* 6590
Christmas Miniatures, Book 1 *(Goldston)* 6903
Christmas Songs & Solos, Book 1 *(Goldston)* 6048
Story of Christmas, The *(Olson)* 800
We Wish You a Merry Christmas *(White-Hayward)* 11743

Late Elementary/Early Intermediate
Christmas Cheer, Book 1 *(Mier)* 6680
Easiest Christmas Carols *(Small)* 660
Merry Little Christmas, A *(Renfrow)* 16883
Nutcracker Suite, The *(Kowalchyk/Lancaster)* 16876

Early Intermediate
Christmas, Christmas, Christmas *(Ray)* 11740
Christmas Festival, Book 4 *(Kowalchyk/Lancaster)* 6599
Christmas Lites—Modern & Bright *(Aaronson)* 11735
Christmas Miniatures, Book 2 *(Goldston)* 14708
Christmas Songs & Solos, Book 2 *(Goldston)* 6591
Simply Christmas *(Ray)* 1188
Something Special for Christmas *(Hartsell)* 6015
We Wish You a Jazzy Christmas *(Rollin)* 16882

Intermediate
Carols for the Season, Organ *(Page)* 12231
Christmas Carol Songbook, The *(Small)* 662
Christmas Cheer, Book 2 *(Mier)* 6697
Christmas from the Heart, Book 1 *(Massoud)* 14695
Christmas from the Heart, Book 2 *(Massoud)* 16879
Christmas Holiday *(Palmer)* 658
Christmas Impressions, Book 1 *(Rollin)* 6566
Christmas Impressions, Book 2 *(Rollin)* 6682
Christmas Pleasures *(Rollin)* 11744
Christmas Silhouettes *(Alexander)* 6006
Christmas to Remember, A *(Hartsell)* 6046
Family Christmas Sing-Along, A *(Ray)* 6687
Gifts of the Season *(Wells)* 18753
Notebook for Saint Nicholas *(Jancewicz)* 18076
Ragtime Christmas, A *(Renfrow)* 18755
Sounds Christmas *(Olson)* 2390
Spotlight on Christmas *(Rollin)* 18761

Intermediate/Late Intermediate
Christmas Inspirations, Book 1 *(Tingley)* 17383
Christmas Kaleidoscope, Book 1 *(Mier)* 16878
Christmas Kaleidoscope, Book 2 *(Mier)* 18754
Christmas Stylings—Modern & Bright, Book 1 *(Aaronson)* 6014
Nutcracker Suite, The *(Kowalchyk/Lancaster)* 6900

Late Intermediate
Christmas Collage, A, Book 1 *(Hartsell)* 6681
Christmas Collage, A, Book 2 *(Hartsell)* 6699
Christmas Collection, A, Book 1 *(Renfrow)* 6047
Christmas Splendor *(Alexander)* 16918

Late Intermediate/Early Advanced
Christmas Collection, A, Book 2 *(Renfrow)* 6549
Christmas Fantasy, A *(Alexander)* 6559
Christmas Stylings—Modern & Bright, Book 2 *(Aaronson)* 6045

Early Advanced
Come to the Manger *(Page)* 14711

Early Advanced/Advanced
Christmas with Style *(Ray)* 659
Mendelssohn – Six Christmas Pieces, Op. 72 *(Palmer)* 1958
More Christmas with Style *(Ray)* 1189
Tchaikovsky – The Nutcracker Suite *(Hinson)* 4856
Variations on Adeste Fidelis *(Taylor/Krauss/Hinson)* 11131

Christmas Duets

Early Elementary
Duets for Christmas Lovers, Book 1 *(Goldston)* 6663

Early Elementary/Elementary
First Favorite Christmas Duets *(Olson)* 863

Elementary
Duets for Christmas Lovers, Book 2 *(Goldston)* 6664
Up on the Housetop *(Goldston)* 5459

Late Elementary
Christmas for Two *(Ray)* 205
Christmas Tree-O!, A (1 Piano, 6 Hands) *(Alexander)* 14515
Duets for Christmas Lovers, Book 3 *(Goldston)* 6665
Holly and the Ivy, The (1 Piano, 6 Hands) *(Alexander)* 14235
'Twas the Night Before... *(Alexander)* 6683

Early Intermediate
Away in a Manger *(Tingley)* 18974
Coventry Carol, The *(Alexander)* 8425
What Child Is This? *(Massoud)* 18975

Intermediate
Carol of the Bells *(Rollin)* 18976
Ding Dong Merrily on High *(Mier)* 18977
Magic of Christmas, The, Book 1 *(Alexander)* 653
Magic of Christmas, The, Book 2 *(Alexander)* 235
Silent Night *(Aaronson)* 18978

Intermediate/Late Intermediate
The Nutcracker Suite for Two *(Rollin)* 16919

Early Advanced
God Rest Ye Merry, Gentlemen *(Alexander)* 18979

Early Advanced/Advanced
Reinecke – Nutcracker and the Mouse King, Op. 46 *(Hinson)* 2275
Tchaikovsky – The Nutcracker Suite *(Hinson)* 4858

Alfred Publishing Co., Inc.
16320 Roscoe Blvd., Suite 100
P.O. Box 10003
Van Nuys, CA 91410-0003

alfred.com

19746 $6.99 i

0 38081 18958
ISBN 0-7390-1329-7

T4-AXP-478

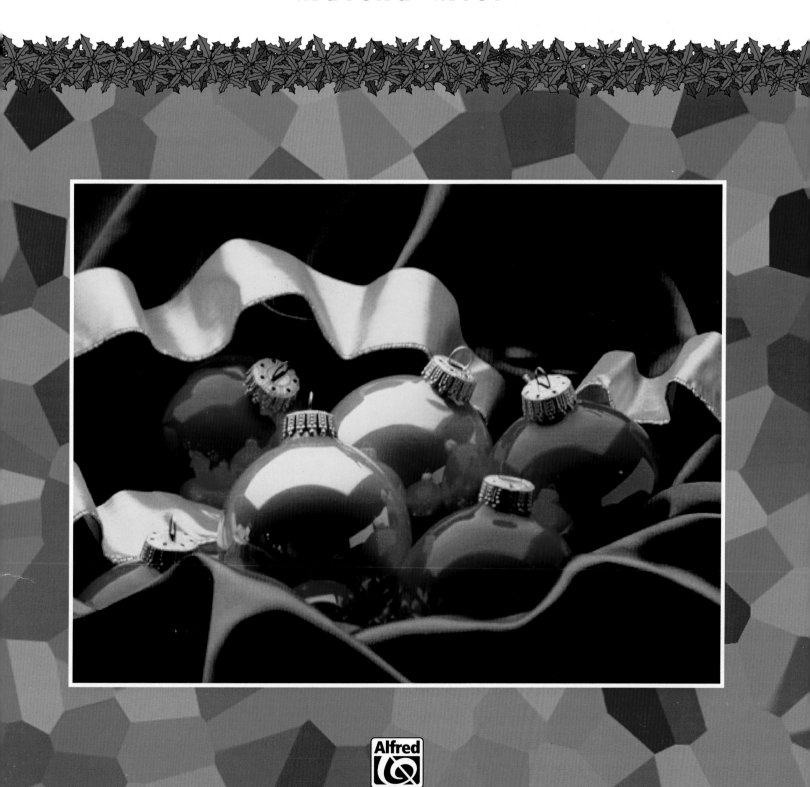